Ariadne's Thread and The ᴍᵧ of Happily Ever After

Beautifully written, clear sighted and practical, this re-vision of the ancient myth of Ariadne's Thread gives "happily ever after" a long overdue rewrite. It provides deep and insightful navigation truths for women who want to explore divergent paths and trust more deeply their own inner authority. Menato's feminine wisdom is a faithful inner and outer guide. Added potency comes from the fact she has clearly lived by what she shares in these pages.

Barbara Cecil, author, co-founder of the women's international leadership program, Coming Into Your Own, and creator of The Symbols Way used by Dialogos, The Presencing Institute and Boeing

Sarah-Jane Menato takes a timeless story and makes it a powerful guide for women's lives today. Through her incisive insight into the deeper narrative of the Ariadne myth, Sarah-Jane compels us to live our lives more fully, take creative action more courageously and hold on to our "thread" more intensely as we journey into the unknown, uncovering new hope as we go.

Sarah Rozenthuler, chartered psychologist, leadership consultant and author of *Life-Changing Conversations*

This compelling narrative reveals how the archetypal themes of the Greek myth of Ariadne, originally framed within a patriarchal culture, can be re-visioned as the journey of a woman who learned to follow her own inner thread through the challenges and transformations in her life. Weaving in her own personal story to great effect, the author describes how this myth can inspire and guide women to be true to themselves and to their deepest instincts.

Clare Martin, author of *Mapping the Psyche*

Ariadne's Thread and The Myth of Happily Ever After

A truth-full account for women navigating timeless and enduring challenges

Ariadne's Thread and The Myth of Happily Ever After

A truth-full account for women navigating timeless and enduring challenges

Sarah-Jane Menato

BOOKS

Winchester, UK
Washington, USA

First published by O-Books, 2018
O-Books is an imprint of John Hunt Publishing Ltd., 3 East St., Alresford,
Hampshire SO24 9EE, UK
office1@jhpbooks.net
www.johnhuntpublishing.com

For distributor details and how to order please visit the 'Ordering' section on our website.

ISBN: 978 1 78535 812 8
978 1 78535 813 5 (ebook)
Library of Congress Control Number: 2017948416

A CIP catalogue record for this book is available from the British Library.

Design: Stuart Davies

Printed and bound by CPI Group (UK) Ltd, Croydon, CR0 4YY, UK

We operate a distinctive and ethical publishing philosophy in
all areas of our business, from our global network of authors to
production and worldwide distribution.

Contents

These pages are dedicated to each woman courageously
following her own Thread through the uncertainties, distortions,
challenges and joys in her everyday life.

A Note To The Reader On The Threshold Of This Book

There is something in every one of you that waits and listens for the sound of the genuine in yourself. It is the only true guide you will ever have. And if you cannot hear it, you will all of your life spend your days on the ends of strings that somebody else pulls.
~ Howard Thurman

While the account in the pages ahead is written, as most stories are, with a beginning, middle and an end, what is shared is unlikely to be reflected so neatly in your own journey. Your current stage of life may place you in the middle of my tale. So skip and skim if you want to… follow your thread. Don't feel obligated to stay with mine.

In these first pages I set some context and explore the ways in which myths can be worked with and why they matter to me. So, go straight to Chapter 1 and the myth of Ariadne and her Thread if you prefer. Find your place, go your own way and use this book in any way you feel to.

This writing emerged as a result of pressure I felt from two directions; an "outer" call from women I work with in my coaching practice, and an "inner" directive to share treasures I surfaced while diving deeply during murky times. I found a whole chest of treasures in the wreck of the ancient myth of Ariadne. And over the years as I brought each barnacle-encrusted piece to the surface, in the sunlight, it became clear to me that Ariadne has an untold story. Her story happens also to be my story and the story of women I work with who successfully cross thresholds at times of major transition in their lives.

Anyone who has successfully crossed a threshold knows that, paradoxically, life as we have known it comes to an end. But we aren't dead, and the mess of our "previous lives" is usually still

1

all around us. How we tend "the remains" of what has ended impacts the future we move into.

It seems as if many aspects of life as we've known it are coming to an end on this planet. If that's true, what happens next may depend, in part, on the trustworthiness of the threads we follow and the truth of the narratives we embrace. Ariadne led me surefooted to an alternative narrative when I faithfully followed her Thread. She has become an ally I will not abandon and she's given me permission to introduce you to her. She is not only pleased to meet you; she's been looking forward to it for a very long time.

Sitting on an exposed shoreline with Ariadne during a particularly windswept time of endings in both our lives, she told me her version of past events. She explained to me that her myth, as we know it in the 21st century (which you will read in full in Chapter 1), doesn't reference the mess left in the Labyrinth once Theseus had slain the Minotaur. It doesn't warn of the toxic aftermath of years of destruction and violence in what had been a sacred space. It doesn't tell the whole story about how, during the time the Minotaur occupied the Labyrinth, there was no sacred darkness in which endings could take place, or new life begin.

Ariadne knows about dealing with the messy "remains" of a previous life even after successfully crossing a major threshold, and leaving an "old" life behind. She explained to me how even after the Minotaur was slain, his rotting carcass remained in the Labyrinth. Ariadne, it seems, began cleaning, but not as we know it. She learned about restoring sacred space that has been violated and she would like me to share her experience. And by the way, she asked me to be sure to tell you that the story we've all heard about her one-night stand on Naxos with Theseus isn't true.

I believe that women today are on a specific threshold with respect to events in the larger world at this time. I believe we have a particular role to play in successfully navigating a time of endings. Women in the Western democratic world have gained many freedoms in recent years. But in some respects, we are as trapped by our cultural paradigm as we ever have been. Reenlisted in epic and endless repeats of versions of "happily ever after" women have not been well served by the all-pervasive narratives we have been raised with.

With life expectancy for women heading for 82 and retirement becoming a thing of the past, by the time we get to be midlife over-50s women, we have an unprecedented opportunity. The majority of us may live long enough for the second half of our lives to be lived from very different inner ground.

Many of us women will live for a considerable number of years beyond childbearing, childrearing, high flying careers and our culture's stereotypes of physical beauty. This presents women with an opportunity to redefine for themselves what has value, worth and the meaning of success. If your definition of success has included breaking the "glass ceiling", you may have found yourself on the other side of it, equal to but no better off than men currently are. Men's dissatisfaction it seems may be "equal" to women's, if perhaps for different reasons.

We live in a patriarchal culture. What is often not taken into account is that it is as toxic for men as it is for women. Patriarchy is not men. It is not even the masculine principle. Patriarchy (in this context) is used as a way to name and describe a system within which both men and women are currently organised. This system happens to give men primacy. It is sometimes assumed that a matriarchy would give women primacy and the imbalances would swing the other way. This is not what is being suggested here; a distinction is being made between masculine and men, and feminine and women.

Life is not a straight trajectory. We do not set off, learn the rules and then live "happily ever after" if we obey them. My experience is that life is more like a spiral on which familiar themes cycle around again and again at each new level. We continually learn and grow throughout our lives and have myriad opportunities to let change happen and step more fully into integrated, whole selves capable of deeper fulfilment and joy.

Authors Angeles Arrien (*The Second Half of Life*) and Louann Brizendine, MD (*The Female Brain*) each in very different ways make cases for biological, spiritual and psychological dimensions to being a woman that coexist and constantly inform each other. Any threshold we arrive at on one level has impact on the other two. Ariadne's thread leads us through life transitions. At each threshold or gateway, we're presented with opportunities to "thresh" our experiences. Time and again we arrive at thresholds where we can take the "gold" out of painful stories, move forward, and leave behind what no longer serves us.

The narratives and once prevalent ideas of both femininity and masculinity are currently under intense scrutiny. The dominant global culture appears to be in a period of breakdown. This has happened before. Our planet has known shattering experiences many times. There is evidence to suggest that not so long ago there were highly civilized, evolved and enlightened cultures. The last remnants of such a culture may have been destroyed just 3,500 years ago by earthquakes and tsunamis not unlike the Boxing Day tsunami we saw on our screens in Indonesia in 2004, and in Japan in 2011, but on a much larger and more devastating scale.

Ancient myths tell of an earth-centred civilization, that vanished, literally shattered by violent earth changes. Pieces of stories and myths from those times endure. They suggest women and men may not always have lived within the patriarchal paradigm we do today. The mythic tale of Ariadne is one thread that comes to us, indicating other major thresholds in a not so distant past.

About Myths, Fairy Tales and Happily Ever After

The word myth has many meanings. It can mean a lie; it can also mean an oral legacy passed down from pre-recorded history. Myths are sometimes seen as history distorted by being passed down, and sometimes as metaphors and allegories for inner processes – stories that are symbolically but not factually "true". All are relevant here.

I've discovered that one of the most important things a woman can do is commit to uncovering her own truth for herself in her life. This involves making important distinctions between the **facts of what she has lived** and the **truth of her own experience** in her daily life. There are lies we must debunk about what it means to be a woman, and what it means to lead successful lives. The version of the stories we ultimately accept for ourselves may determine not just our personal experience but also the larger story unfolding globally.

There is a quote you will have heard: "The whole is greater than the sum of its parts."[1] I recently learned this is a misquote and an example of a story unhinged from its original meaning which gets lost in translation and retelling. Many mythic themes relating to The Feminine have similarly become separated from their original meaning. Ariadne, the Labyrinth, the Minotaur, and Theseus is one example. In the bones of myths there is, however, always a shining truth. The misquote "The whole is greater than the sum of its parts" is no exception.

Kurt Koffka (1886 to 1941) was a Gestalt psychologist. He made the original observation from which has come our current day lie about the whole being greater than the sum of its parts. Apparently what Kurt Koffka originally said was: "The whole is **other** than the sum of its parts." He did not like the English translation and firmly corrected his students if they substituted "greater" for "other". He apparently would say: "This is not a principle of addition." What did he mean? What is the deeper truth he was pointing to? And no matter how many people

5

believe the version we're all familiar with, that doesn't make it true.

As a woman, the version I internalise of what Kurt Koffka said supports either a principle of addition that's required because I am "less than" and must add to and fix to become "greater", or the possibility that by accepting and including all of my parts I step into an "other" experience of myself. I am not interested in becoming a greater version of the leadership we currently see in the world. I want to be entirely "other". I am not interested in striving and efforting to be "equal". I am interested and committed to "other".

"Other" is hard to pin down. It includes a profound experience we're privileged to know in ways that are deeply personal, but relates also to universal and mythic shared themes of being present to the deepest truth in any given moment. **The deepest truth of who we each are is *other* than the sum of the *facts* of what has happened to us.** There is a matrix of wholeness that undergirds what has been disabled in our culture with respect to The Feminine. We are in the process of enablement through radical inclusion of all of ourselves, not fixing.

One of the most toxic and pervasive lies is that as women, we need "fixing". What might happen if we held a moratorium on "fixing"? What would happen if we replaced "fixing" with radical "inclusion" of ourselves exactly as we are? What if the cutting edge for women's personal, professional and leadership development in the 21st century is radical inclusion of our selves just the way we are? What happens if I say: There is nothing wrong with you. You have everything you need; simply include it. Include all of yourself; the disabled parts, the broken parts, the unfinished parts, the disowned parts, the terrifying parts.

Given that there are currently no models of entirely effective, inclusive, integrated feminine leadership, how can we know which bits of ourselves to leave behind? If we accept we don't know, wouldn't it make sense not to slice off, lock up, make up, fold up or tuck away any parts of ourselves? We are going into the unknown. Don't prejudge parts of yourself simply because they haven't been useful (yet). Our judgements about our own (and others') underused, undeveloped and possibly misused capacities cost us dearly. Myths can help.

The Olympic Games are rooted in myth and archetypes. I was drawn to the Paralympic Games in 2016 because of my reflections at that time about "disabled" parts of ourselves. If we are disabled in some ways, that's a fact, and just the way it is. But that fact isn't necessarily the same as the truth of personal experience. With that understanding comes permission to engage with the full current of our own life-force moving through us now, just the way we are. That's an experience of "other".

When the fullness of life is given permission to flow through us, exactly the way we are, we experience the sum of our parts being "other". We are both disabled and perfectly formed for our unique work. Both are true at the same time. We have nothing to hide and nothing to apologise for. This is a big deal for women in visible leadership roles.

Our gifts and energy are waiting to flow in our lives. But the switch is "off" if we accept an unhelpful edge that personal and leadership development can have if we interpret inner work as a need to fix troublesome aspects of ourselves as women in order to become "greater". It is my increasing experience in my work that it is time to come fully into our own in a "whole" new way, accepting the broken, damaged parts and our "disabilities". The "on" switch is risk. The risk to let our life-force move through us now, exactly the way we are. When we do that, the magic of "Other" happens.

The whole of a myth is "other" than the sum of the parts

A whole Myth can be a way of opening to a deeply personal experience of "other" when the person hearing or reading the story includes all the complex characters and her relationship to each of them. Myths allow us to examine powerful personal themes one step removed, leaving our own vulnerabilities protected. Usually, but not always, we're drawn to a particular myth or story because of identification with the central character. Different myths have different themes and we likely resonate with stories that speak to our own core issues.

The myth of Ariadne is, for me, the overarching story of what we face as women, within current dominant cultural norms. Working any myth, over time, reveals aspects of ourselves in all the archetypes in the same, single myth. This is a different take on radical inner inclusivity and diversity. If I can own all the parts of the stories I tell, what impact might that have? This is one route to the experience of the whole of me being "other" than the sum of my parts. It's certainly the magic occasionally present in a great story.

Sharing our real life stories with women who have stories like our own may feel comforting but ultimately may not be helpful. We often choose to connect with women who have real life stories like our own and exclude those who don't. If we do that, the deeper experience of shared meaning likely remains elusive. This is because our individual stories as women, the biographical details, are specific about **"how"** something happened to us. But collectively there is a **"what"** that has happened to us, all of us, in all of our lives. **"How"** things happen can separate us, **"what"** has happened is the common thread that unites us. If we can get beyond judgements of the biographical details, we begin to powerfully connect in new ways to new ground we share and can build on together.

To take advantage of the magic in myth requires alertness to more than one level of our experience at the same time. We have to be willing to sit on an edge and to hold on and let go at the same time. We have to hold on to the truth of our own experience and let go of attachment to the past and stories about it that don't serve us. What to hold on to and what to let go of comes with practice, trust and, increasingly, the support of other women committed to listening to "the sound of the genuine".

American philosopher and civil rights leader Howard Thurman said: "There is something in every one of you that waits and listens for the sound of the genuine in yourself. It is the only true guide you will ever have. And if you cannot hear it, you will all of your life spend your days on the ends of strings that somebody else pulls." In all stories we can learn to listen beyond the details and facts of "how" something happened to the deeper truth of "what" happened; the truth of personal experience.

All cultures have oral histories that pass from generation to generation. There is truth in them even if the original facts are obscured. A myth is something that could be said to be true but not necessarily factual. It's true on the inside but not necessarily factually accurate on the outside. What if we've mistakenly taken the outside of the "happily ever after" story as our blueprint while failing to look inside the story for the truth of what is being revealed?

Myths, symbols, archetypes and metaphors allow us to gently approach ourselves without scaring ourselves away. If we are drawn to a myth because we identify with the main character, what might happen if we turn our attention in new ways and find out what the other characters have to show us? What do things look and feel like from their perspectives? Can they give us insight into the parts of ourselves we may have tried to fix or disown?

Culturally women traditionally tend to take responsibility for all the people in their extended external lives. My invitation as we share Ariadne's story is to consider taking responsibility for all the characters in our inner dramas. If our central, strongest sense of self isn't balanced by all the other parts of ourselves in life, one aspect of our identity can take over, dominate and can, at the very least, limit our experience. At the other extreme, it can derail the show.

The story of Ariadne contains the vital players and a star-studded cast easily recognised from our "outer" lives. Ariadne's story also suggests a map and provides evidence to support our instinctive sense that there is a sustainable way forward for ourselves and our planet at this complex time. Could it be that the way forward is led by following Ariadne's Thread, an inner Feminine commitment to live lives faithful to deep truth rather than the facts of the external prevailing paradigm? A reorientation of authority from exterior to interior is, it would seem, underway.

Hundreds of years of retelling familiar myths and fairy tales in our predominant culture of patriarchy has very effectively smothered The Feminine. It isn't possible to unpick what has happened in the past that led to the current pervasive lie of "happily ever after", without understanding that the versions of familiar myths and fairy tales we have grown up with (and continue to hear) all have the overlay of our cultural, patriarchal paradigm. Under the overlay, deeply buried, is the truth of "happily ever after". If attempts are made to address only the stereotypes in current versions of fairy tales and myths by rewriting them, the road back through them to the archetypal power of The Feminine and the truth in the ancient tales is covered over and risks being lost.

Gender-reversal versions of fairy tales or added backstories to extant myths don't ultimately serve us because the accuracy of the metaphors, symbols and archetypes get muddled (at best) and sidelined. Classic fairy tales such as *Sleeping Beauty*, *Cinderella*, *Snow White* and *The Little Mermaid* all have deep archetypal truth buried beneath the increasingly unacceptable stereotypes the main characters have become. But care should be taken not to throw the baby out with the bathwater by just rewriting stories.

Modern stories are free to effectively dismantle gender stereotypes and Disney (and other) examples include *101 Dalmatians, Frozen, Happy Feet, Toy Story 2* and *Monsters vs. Aliens*. While these modern stories deal a welcome blow to gender stereotyping, what they can't do is connect to the power available to young girls in the Archetypes in the classic ancient myths and fairy tales. Both the modern new stories and the classic ancient are needed.

The ground of fairy tales and ancient myth can't be stepped over or we end up with one-dimensional versions of the multidimensional reality of being human and, in this case, of being a woman. Every myth or fairy tale addresses different aspects of The Feminine. Equally, each woman has her own unique life to lead and personal work to do. You may find your myth will call you and help you do your work. The myth of Ariadne called to me and I have faithfully followed her thread. Here is the version I first heard.

Chapter 1

The Myth of Ariadne and her Thread

The story of Ariadne and her Thread opens on what is today the northern coast of the Island of Crete in what is now the municipality of Heraklion. You can go there if you want to. In Ariadne's time, the island was ruled by her father, Old King Minos, and she lived in what came to be known as the famous Palace of Knossos. Ariadne was very much her father's daughter, and a princess. In the story as it has been told to us, there is no mention of a Queen at the side of Old King Minos, or a Mother for Ariadne.

Under the vast and exquisite expanse of cool marble floors in what came to be known as the Palace of Knossos, deep beneath the surface, there stretched a vast, dark Labyrinth. At the very centre of the Labyrinth was the lair of a fearsome creature, half man and half bull, known as The Minotaur. The Minotaur inhabited the Labyrinth, and anyone who entered his convoluted domain just below the surface of everyday life never came out. Many tried, but they all lost their way and once disoriented in the terrifying darkness and complexity of the Labyrinth they were slain and devoured by the monstrous Minotaur. Ariadne lived her life above the Labyrinth on the surface of this invisible but ever-present force each and every day.

Ariadne grew up in the palace with the terrorizing force of The Minotaur below her every step. She slept above it, ate above it and played above it each and every day of her life. It was just the way things were and Ariadne never questioned the norms of her father's kingdom. Over the years Ariadne the girl became a young woman, and one day as Ariadne watched the familiar comings and goings of daily life in her father's kingdom, she noticed the arrival of a ship from Athens. Ariadne's attention remained on the ship as it docked in the port. Before long, a handsome young man called Theseus stepped off his swift sailing ship and as he set foot on the island, something dramatic shifted in Ariadne. She was on the threshold of change.

Theseus was the son of the King of Athens, and had come across the sea from his father's kingdom as part of an annual ritual. Each and every year for all the years of her life, Ariadne had witnessed a procession of the seven most promising youths from Athens arriving on Crete in order to challenge the Minotaur. The strongest, most beautiful, athletic and intelligent youths were selected and sent to Crete from Athens. If, as always happened, they failed to slay the fearsome Minotaur, their lives served as sacrifice in the Labyrinth to appease the dark forces within it. Ariadne grew up in her father's kingdom on Crete watching this pattern repeat. Year after year youth, beauty, strength, vitality, virility and intelligence were sacrificed. It was simply the way things were.

The young princess Ariadne gazed out at Theseus. She was taken both by what she saw physically and by his stated determination to slay the Minotaur. But Ariadne had seen all this before; she knew how the ritual unfolded each and every year. And as she watched the pattern repeat again, something flickered in Ariadne. This year, somehow, it felt different. Deep in Ariadne was a sense of something she felt compelled to pay attention to, and as she followed her intuition, a plan emerged in her thinking of how she could save Theseus and get something she began to realise she wanted for herself.

Ariadne came up with a very simple strategy and proposed a deal to Theseus; it was a pact between them. Ariadne offered to help Theseus slay the Minotaur and find his way safely back out of the terrifying Labyrinth if he in turn would promise to take her with him, when he sailed away from her father's kingdom in his ship. Theseus agreed.

On the appointed day of the "ritual" sacrifice of the seven youths from Athens, Ariadne gave Theseus a ball of thread. She explained to him carefully and precisely how to unravel the thread as he walked into the Labyrinth. She promised she would hold tight to the other end so that as he journeyed deeper and deeper through the absolute darkness, Ariadne's Thread would remain securely in place to ensure Theseus was oriented in a safe, secure connection to her out in the

13

lighted world. He was to slay the Minotaur and then follow Ariadne's Thread back out. This is exactly what happened. Theseus went into the Labyrinth, triumphed over the fearsome Minotaur and followed Ariadne's Thread back out to safety.

Defying her father, the Old King Minos, Ariadne and Theseus fled together on his swift Athenian sailing ship over the water and away from all that Ariadne had known. Ariadne left her father's house behind her. The two young royals sailed towards an island called Naxos where the ship weighed anchor and they spent the night on the shores of the island. The next morning when Ariadne woke up on Naxos, she found Theseus had gone. She saw him and his ship in the distance sailing off, vanishing over the sea. Ariadne was alone on the beach; she had brought nothing with her and stood in everything she possessed. She was alone in territory that was alien to her.

The story as it is told today portrays Ariadne as isolated and grief-stricken, feeling abandoned and her trust in the promise Theseus had made to her betrayed. Ariadne was left standing on unknown ground. The past was gone and the future she may have begun to imagine for herself had sailed off without her. What happens next in the story is dramatic. As Ariadne waved and wept, hoping it was all a mistake and trying to catch the attention of the retreating Theseus and as his ship vanished over the horizon, she sensed something behind her. Ariadne turned her head and as she did so, not from the sea or the direction from which she had come, but from inland, from an unknown landscape she hadn't been aware of, or paid any attention to, a chariot arrived. Out of the chariot leaped the Greek god, Dionysus.

While Theseus may have been the son of the King of Athens, and royal, he was still a mere mortal. Dionysus, however, was a god. This part of the story, as it has been told down through the ages, concludes with Dionysus and Ariadne falling in love. He crowns her with a circlet of stars and, mutually devoted, they marry, establish an eternal loving bond allowing them, as the story goes, to live happily ever after.

Chapter 2

Deconstructing the Myth

The myth of "happily ever after" lives on, but the shattered truth behind the myth remains, for the most part, lost. Scattered pieces lie, like a broken plate, all around. To begin to see the whole undistorted picture, we'll need to pick up one piece at time and be willing to hold it up to the light. Any piece of this story, reflected on with courage, has the potential to reveal what we sense must surely be there.

I am not a Jungian analyst or an anthropologist, I have no relevant academic credentials; I am not a recognised "expert". In this patriarchal culture, feminine authority gained in the trenches of life experience doesn't come with credentials, qualifications, public recognition or money. However, that is no indication of value or worth. **The willingness to act without the need for validation or permission from current mainstream definitions of authority and success is a profoundly needed feminine stance.** So here I am with my twenty-first century version of taking action (as Ariadne did) in the kingdom ruled by Old King Minos. You will have your own. It's not that qualifications and academic credentials don't have their place. They certainly do. But this is a story about the Feminine authority of experiential knowing, of gnosis.

Each time I begin to write this section, I float off and drift. My sails empty of even the slightest breeze. No movement. My powerful initial sense of direction and purposeful excitement deflates, and my attention wanes. This may be familiar to you and happens to many of us when we have something creative to birth that is uniquely our own. **And this is the point of this story; I must stay true and follow my Thread.** As I take each next step my inner Ariadne is empowered and my inner Theseus is enlisted for his sailing skills and tools. He will get me from here to the new ground I can't see yet, a finished manuscript. Slowly Theseus learns to act in support of my work, my projects, and my talent. This is very different to his training and previous job description in the kingdom of Old King Minos. **In the "old kingdom", Theseus is accustomed to acting to get something rather than supporting Ariadne to birth something.**

In this way, Theseus and Ariadne must learn to work together as I make my way in the dark and reclaim the Labyrinth. As I write, my inner King Minos regularly suggests I am not qualified and have nothing to write about. If I listen, my creativity is thrown to the Minotaur. Like Ariadne, holding on to my Thread each day, I make a simple plan and keep moving with this story, her story and mine. Word by word my journey with this writing is no different than Ariadne's. Holding on to her Thread, I am assured I will emerge safely and the Minotaur has no predatory power over my "entelechant" action as I write.

I made up the word "entelechant" from the word entelechy which I understand to mean the innate energy in each of us that wants to pull us towards our own fruition. Every seed has entelechy and is why a hyacinth grows to be a hyacinth not a daffodil. It's why you are you and I am me. It's also true that where a daffodil is planted and the care it receives (biography) make a difference to its ability to become fully itself. But biologically, it can only become a daffodil.

"Entelechant" action is Feminine action and the story of Ariadne is about taking action in ways that enable women to come into their own, as fully as the reality of their circumstances allow. If a woman pays attention to her inner Ariadne and holds on to her Thread, Theseus is enlisted and takes "entelechant" action on behalf of a future they mature into together. But each has their own journey. We know much more about the Hero's Journey. Ariadne's story is the Heroine's Journey and is more pilgrimage than adventure.

Ariadne's Thread connects Theseus and Ariadne and they remain connected. Even as their work to mature differentiates and takes Theseus on his own journey while Ariadne remains on Naxos, in this myth Ariadne remains a conscious participant. In the fairy tale of *Sleeping Beauty*, the princess sleeps through the whole story. The prince is maturing and on a journey but Sleeping Beauty wakes up as unconscious and immature as she was at the start of the story. Not so Ariadne. She is a full participant and not only engages in her own journey, she initiates it.

Ways to describe The Feminine might include: a life-giving environment, a birthplace and the matrix of Creation. Without embodied grounding in The Feminine nothing new can be birthed. Having children is a very limited interpretation of this. The ability to birth new ideas, ways of seeing and thinking and taking action from a connected, whole perspective that brings and supports life-flow is included in what is intended here as The Feminine.

There are four principal phases in the story of Ariadne and her Thread. In the myth, these phases take place neatly one after the other. However, in human life, the phases in Ariadne's story usually don't happen sequentially, or in one neat sweep. Ariadne's story spirals through each age and stage of women's lives. The invitation here is to listen for what's true for you. Think of the four phases as signposts, an outline that's not quite yet a map of territory we all navigate in unique ways. We are exploring this together and no one is an expert. Your or my experience can't be wrong, it's just partial. Keep going. Our personal strengths develop as a result of experience gained moving through this landscape.

In time, our shared experiences will reveal what's been there all along. During shattering cycles when everything seems lost, we're left with what we've always had. The simple bones of the Myth are clear and shining. But we have to find them through the tangle we've got into with the Thread of connection and relationship in the current cultural context. Deeply personal threads of sacrifice, loss, betrayal and abandonment in outer relationship have to be untangled to form a sturdy, secure connection and an inner unique marriage of Masculine and Feminine in each of us.

Phase One

Sensing and following inner guidance

Ariadne is a young adult as her story opens on Crete. She's gone through adolescence and the biological upheaval we each go through as girls stepping into the fertility cycle. During that time our brains develop capacity to reason and make informed choices alongside the deep connection to hormones and instincts. Ariadne's sexual identity is emerging; she has "come of age" and is no longer a child.

Ariadne recognised she was in an environment that wasn't safe for a girl stepping on to the fertility cycle and into her emerging sexuality (more about that later). So she came up with a plan and proposed it to Theseus. Many women can point to an external Theseus, a real life person during a tender time with whom a deal was made, a promise, that ended in an experience of betrayal and abandonment. But what if Theseus represents not only an outer real life experience we've factually had, but also an inner archetype of the immature Masculine with a truth to gift us? He invites us to reflect; how have we lived up to promises and commitments we have made to our inner Ariadne, our as yet immature Feminine archetype of "Maiden"? If the arrival of Theseus represents a life stage in the inner world of all young women who are waking to the stirring of future calling, how faithful have we been to that calling? How supported have we felt by our **inner** culture to stay connected and faithful to our own calling?

For Ariadne then, just as it is today, this is an "unsafe" and extremely risky time. Sadly, not much has changed since Ariadne's times. Young women awakening to their sexual nature continue to be in danger. In this biological time of upheaval and transition, Ariadne looks around her needing something she cannot find. Psychologist and author Janet Surrey calls what Ariadne is looking for "relationship authenticity". Ideally young women experience relationship authenticity with their mothers and also find it in other respected role models of the mature "Mother" archetype in their cultures. It is this authentic connection that builds self-esteem and self-worth in young women. But Ariadne's mother is missing.

Looking about her, Ariadne sees no role models of sexually mature, healthy, authentic women (we'll come to Ariadne's Mother, Pasiphae, later). And to make things even more terrifying, each year the most vital and beautiful youths are sacrificed to the Minotaur. What would become of Ariadne if she stepped into everything she knows in her heart she is? She senses correctly, this is not a safe environment in which to come into her own. She senses she will not survive if she stays in the environment that she is, in part, a product of. Ariadne listens to her instincts and follows inner guidance to get away.

In many myths, "mother" is missing for one reason or another. The myth of Ariadne can be seen as the struggle of all women in our culture to connect with an authentic relationship with The Feminine. While our culture places value on certain aspects of motherhood, it excludes others. It can be challenging for women to be authentic about the experience of being a mother.

"Relationship authenticity" doesn't mean a woman providing authenticity has to be perfect. It means she has to be meaningfully connected to the "sound of the genuine" and what is authentic for herself. She can make mistakes, she can get things wrong. An authentic woman dealing with the consequences of her choices cleanly provides an example of womanhood that sets girls free to find out what works for them. It gives young girls the confidence to follow the sound of what is authentic and genuine in themselves and permission to make their own mistakes. While things may not be easy, they will be meaningful and fulfilling.

Louann Brizendine in her book *The Female Brain* notes during puberty a hormone-driven shift to a major interest in sexual attractiveness. Down through recorded history, this has regularly been a perilous time and it was true for Ariadne. According to a major survey of 14-year-olds carried out for the Department for Education, depression and anxiety have risen among teenage girls in England.[2] The report highlights the prevalence of smartphone ownership and social networking, and their impact on young women's developing sexuality. There are new issues for this generation that intensify dynamics that have historically been present at this age for young women. For teenage girls in present day culture dealing with "sexting", pornography and relationship platforms such as Tinder are an everyday reality. The Minotaur is alive and well in 2017.

These present day external dangers are every bit as toxic as the ones Ariadne had to deal with. Ariadne's experience is familiar and, between then and now, all women have negotiated this stage with varying degrees of "authentic" relationship to any external support which would build self-worth and self-esteem. **Here is the first major difference we can make for each other as women.** Authentic relationship and safe places to learn and discover more about the power of connection to our own authentic selves builds solid ground in women. We need these spaces and we need authentic women, not perfect women. We are also all so different.

When I first came across Ariadne and shared her story with a close friend, my friend declared she had absolutely no sense of identification to Ariadne. It was to Theseus sailing off in his ship after slaying the Minotaur and "rescuing" Ariadne that she related. This difference as friends in identification with a shared story first showed me the myth's potential. All the characters are part of the diverse experience of being a woman, not just the central figure of Ariadne.

I identified intensely and immediately with Ariadne and what I interpreted at that time in my life as the experience of being abandoned and betrayed on the beach at Naxos by Theseus. My (female) friend identified with Theseus, fearless, capable and setting off on his next adventure rather than (from my friend's perspective) a helpless, pathetic and naïve Ariadne who should have learned to sail her own damn ship. There are many ways to talk about the Masculine and Feminine balance in our own unique experiences as women. This story, our story, is not about men and women. And so often, as evidenced in the way my friend and I first looked at this myth, it's about stereotypes, not archetypes.

Ten years on, and my friend and I continue to work these self-identified stereotypes in ourselves and our friendship to this day. We've each internalised them differently. But stepping into the archetypes and out of stereotypical projections, I am more comfortably and deeply connected in my kinship and relationship to the archetype of Theseus. My friend has grown and developed her own authentic rootedness in the archetype of Ariadne. Our friendship has supported this. Over the years I have helped my friend consider her relationship to her inner Ariadne and her connection to self and others. My friend has helped me understand and engage with my inner Theseus, and the way I take action on behalf of my own sense of my work in the outer world.

We have both watched each other learn to engage with Theseus on our own terms, rather than those of Old King Minos. Equally we have had to renegotiate our relationships to Ariadne and to engage with her on our own terms, not those of Old King Minos. We are very different women, but one myth contains metaphors for both our journeys and truths even though our life experiences are very different. This appreciation of our different biographies is an example of work women can do to strengthen each other's connection to archetypes and dismantle the stereotypes as we each establish our own unique balance of Masculine and Feminine in ourselves.

A brief word here about archetypes and stereotypes might be helpful. There is more to follow later. In this context, an archetype is an original building block in the psyche present in all people. When accessed and integrated, an archetype is strengthening and empowering. A stereotype could be described as an outer collection of characteristics and clichés. It is usually used to diminish and disempower by perpetuating an image that isn't accurate.

Back to the Myth and Ariadne's Thread

As a way to gently explore our varied and often wildly differing experiences as women, we can reflect on the way we "took our leave", as Ariadne did, at the beginning of the myth. On the Island of Crete, Ariadne is culturally of age to leave home. There are many ways in which young women leave home. Thinking back to your own experience of leaving home, how did it happen?

In an ideal world, young women would leave home with a strong sense of self and move out on an inner initiating impulse of their own towards something they love. In the myth, Ariadne wants to leave home, she's ready. Importantly, although she doesn't know where she wants to go, or what she wants to be, she is firmly connected to her "Thread".

A young woman who arrives at eighteen so well connected to her Thread that she "leaves home" to move towards something she loves, rather than to get away from something, has an advantage. But whatever the manner of our leave-taking, Ariadne's Thread is a symbol of our connection to a sense of self that anchors us. It is well differentiated from what is outside of us, and holds us steady against the pressures that inevitably pull and tug from the prevailing external paradigm.

As human beings we're more likely to invest in ourselves for one of two reasons; either to move towards something we want, or to get away from pain. To move away from "the known" one of these two factors is likely to be strongly at work. Leaving what we know behind is never easy, even when we want to. It is all the more challenging if we haven't "chosen" the change in our circumstances.

Questions to help you use the myth to reflect on your own experience:

Close your eyes and drop your attention into your body. Thinking about your own experience of "leaving home":

1. What were you leaving home to get away from?
2. What were you moving towards when you left home?
3. When you think about what you were getting away from, do you notice any sensation in your body?
4. When you think about what you were moving towards, do you notice any sensation in your body?
5. If your "emotional intelligence" could speak, what might it have to say about what you experienced "leaving home"?
6. Does your heart or body have an intuitive message to convey to you in the here and now, at this juncture in your present day life?

Phase Two

Standing back, seeing patterns, making a plan and moving through fear

Taking steps into "the unknown" requires moving through fear even if we are heading towards something we have chosen. **Part one** of Ariadne's journey began with listening to and taking seriously her intuition, instinctively knowing something different was needed, and being present and open to what came next. She followed her gut instinct. **Part two** is about standing back, emotionally detaching from the feelings that triggered the desire to take action, verifying inner perceptions with outer evidence, and watching and waiting for opportunity. It's strategic. Ariadne doesn't leap into action; she holds the impulse to act while she looks around her for possible external support and confirmation of what she has sensed intuitively.

In the myth, Ariadne chooses to leave. She knows she is ready. She is alert and watching for an opportunity. She knows she has to do something but she doesn't know what or how. Initially she doesn't have a plan, but just because she doesn't know "how" it doesn't mean she "can't". She has much to learn, and untapped resources to access. She's going to grow into her next step.

Along comes Theseus in his sailing ship and Ariadne's perspective on her situation shifts. Until this point, the sea around the island has prevented her from leaving. Now, with her emerging plan, the sea looks suddenly very different. It provides her with a way out if she can access new resources and the right tools: in this case, sailing skills and a ship.

The sooner we learn to follow Ariadne's Thread the better because usually there's greater flexibility and less at stake in our lives the younger we are. The sooner we learn there is no rule book, no secret code, nothing that will protect us from pain, loss and heartache, the sooner we're free to engage with the messy reality of an authentic, full and rich life where there are no guarantees. Stepping off the well-worn tracks of social and cultural norms takes tremendous courage. Young Ariadne has this.

There is no Queen beside her father, the King. No clearer statement could be made: there is no place for the mature Feminine in his kingdom. This should sound warning bells that alert us. But so many women in so many stories sleep through the warning bells. Fortunately Ariadne and her Thread are always poised within us, waiting for us to feel and listen. Ariadne can get quite loud within us as she really doesn't want to remain a princess.

While there is no mention in this myth of the absent Queen, Ariadne like all of us had a mother. Her name was Pasiphae, and she was the daughter of Helios, the Sun himself. What happened to Pasiphae has everything to do with the danger Ariadne intuits and the patterns she perceives in her father's kingdom. Growing up in the palace Ariadne never questioned the way things were. Except one day, when she was the same age as the golden youths sent from Athens, something shifted.

Ariadne becomes conscious, she wakes up to the cultural rituals, patterns and contracts in the prevailing culture that are not going to serve her. She suddenly sees what's been there all along. There is no mature Feminine in her father's kingdom. Where is the Queen? And why does no one speak up as the strongest, most beautiful, athletic and intelligent youths in their physical prime are sacrificed in the Labyrinth year after year?

The Minotaur is the usurper at our core where worthiness should live in us as women. In a patriarchal system, suppressed and enraged this imprisoned energy takes on a monstrous, terrifying and devouring nature. With the complicity of the kingdom, the best, the strongest and most beautiful never come into their own.

This is the energy of the absent feminine; distorted, suppressed and enraged. When the prevailing dominant paradigm, patriarchy, not only doesn't permit equality, but actively imposes dependency, silence and submission, The Feminine is oppressed. The Minotaur is what every woman fears she could be labelled if she were to speak up, stand up and be counted. Fear of offending the dominant paradigm, personified by Old King Minos, can silence a young woman. Even if she doesn't know why or understand the background, she senses there is a story that isn't being told. Something vital is not permitted above ground, let alone given an equal place on a throne beside the king.

When the maturing Feminine nature becomes a threat to the status quo it is banished below to starve. Not having what it needs to survive, the suppressed feminine becomes a dark predator of epic proportions. Ariadne starts to see the way things are.

Jungian analyst and writer Jean Bolen uses Greek mythology to give readers insight into psychological archetypes of The Feminine as well as "shadow parts" of undeveloped, split off, unintegrated aspects of The Feminine.[3] These neglected and suppressed aspects give indication of the power of the Minotaur.

Growing up, Ariadne has watched whatever had the power and potential to bring change, or challenge the status quo, killed off seasonally. Maturity, strength and beauty in mature women are nowhere to be seen. This is not a safe environment for a young girl on the threshold of major personal transition. So, one day when she's ready, a combination of her outer circumstances and inner biological and psychological readiness, Ariadne comes up with and proposes a plan of action. The plan is simple; the proposal is clear and a deal is agreed. She'll save Theseus if he will take her away from the island when he leaves. He agrees.

Questions to help you use the myth to think about your own experience:

1. Reading Ariadne's story, at this point in her life is there anything that looks or feels familiar to you in yours?

2. In your own life, have you been at any of the junctures Ariadne stood at?

3. Are there any habits, patterns or cycles in your own experience that you have become aware of and chose to break?

4. Are there any patterns in your own experience that you have yet to address?

Phase Three

No one is coming

Taking action on our own behalf and moving through anger

Sometimes women today learn to use anger to defend and take action on behalf of their children. Culturally it's acceptable for a woman to be strong for her children. But when she tries to use that same inner capacity in service of her own "work" in the world, it's often another matter. Taking action on her own behalf is what Ariadne does next.

After having made external connections that support her to stay true to her inner intuitive Thread, she takes action on her own behalf. Step by step, Ariadne shows us how to move effectively through a creative process. In part one, she listens to her intuition and takes seriously what she intuits. But she doesn't act yet. In part two she steps back from her feelings, and watches and waits until she can see how the outer patterns and underlying cycles reflect and inform her inner intuitive impulse. But she doesn't act yet. From this strategic place she also thinks about things from the perspective of Theseus. Understanding what he wants enables Ariadne to come up with, and propose, a win-win plan. Then, and only then, does she put her plan into action. She cooperates and collaborates. She doesn't dominate or manipulate. The deal is clear, conscious and explicit.

The timing is right and the moment Ariadne has planned and waited for arrives. On the day of the "ritual" sacrifice of the seven youths, part three of our story unfolds and Ariadne takes action. It's important to note that Ariadne's original impulse was to take action on her own behalf to get herself away from her father's kingdom. It was not about Theseus. It was about Ariadne herself. She had her own purpose. While Theseus was a part of her plan, he wasn't her focus. Important also to underline what the contract was. They made a bargain. Theseus signed up because Ariadne said she would get him out of the Labyrinth alive. In return she asked him to take her away. He agreed. The deal was explicit, conscious and clear.

The story that then unfolds can be told and interpreted in so many ways depending on our cultural perspectives and stereotypical biases. It can be told with a bias that makes it about Ariadne "helping" Theseus. It can be told with a bias that makes it about Ariadne falling in love with and wanting Theseus. But looking again, we remember: Ariadne's initial instinct, and the motivation for the whole plan, was to take action on her own behalf and get away from a situation that endangered her ongoing growth and maturity beyond Maiden archetype to fertile, powerful life-giving Mother.

In the current day telling of this myth, Ariadne goes out of the frying pan and into the fire. With the bias of current day stereotypes, "helpful" Ariadne is abandoned and betrayed by Theseus after a one-night stand on the beach. But there are ways to tell this story without the overlay of longing for the hero-saviour to come to the rescue.

Let's remember that this was Ariadne's plan. Could it be that the myth is clearly showing us how Ariadne and Theseus did exactly what they were supposed to do for each other? They connected the Masculine and Feminine principle with The Thread that enabled them to work together exactly as they are designed to do. When the contract is clear and the deal conscious, this powerful partnership serves and saves them both. Could it be that in the morning, Ariadne waves goodbye and looks forward to the next phase of her own journey as Theseus sails off on his? Remember this is a myth about inner archetypes not outer stereotypes.

In current day telling of this story, we have a tangled mess that forgets this is a myth and a story that's true on the inside, not the outside. It tells an inside-out version of Ariadne abandoned and betrayed by Theseus which perpetuates the ways in which women have been giving part of themselves away ever since. We can take it back. We can remember that Ariadne's Thread is her own. We can remember that her plan to use her Thread to get away is her own. Ariadne took action on her own behalf. The result will be that she finds new ground on which to build an alternative future.

When Ariadne set sail from Crete with Theseus, they left behind them the Labyrinth. They have been true to their words, and built trust and a connection that will endure and individual strengths they will continue to draw on. But when they left Crete together, against the will of Old King Minos, within the Labyrinth lay the remains of the Minotaur. The impact of years of violence, fear and shame relating to the absent Queen did not magically vanish. Clean up was left for another day and is work Ariadne and Theseus will tend to individually over the coming and ongoing cycle. The Minotaur is dead, but the Labyrinth, powerful symbol of The Feminine, has not yet been reclaimed.

Ariadne will learn to live on the shifting sands of the shoreline of Naxos, the not yet solid ground of her own realm. This new realm will emerge in time from the embodied knowing of the Feminine and Masculine working together. Theseus in turn will learn to continue his work as he sails the sea. He knows he would be dead if it wasn't for Ariadne and her thread. And he is now anchored in his experience of connection to Ariadne's Thread rather than in the old paradigm of both their fathers.

The Hero's Journey and the Heroine's Journey are different. Ariadne and Theseus have separate work to do as their lives move forward. Because we are each a unique balance of both masculine and feminine, in a lifetime, we would rightly expect to undertake aspects of both the Hero's and the Heroine's Journeys. To add another challenge to our work as women, in our culture, the Hero's Journey is more widely acknowledged and undertaken by both men and women. The Heroine's Journey is poorly understood and very undervalued. But it is the work Ariadne has to do on the beach. She's not just going to sleep through the next cycle waiting for someone to save her.

About the Labyrinth and the story of Ariadne's mother, a powerful woman indeed

In the most ancient stories across many cultures, a labyrinth is a symbol of The Feminine and the journey or pilgrimage through birth to death and rebirth. The centre of a labyrinth is the place of both death and rebirth. This is the domain of the Great Mother, the mature Feminine in all her life-giving and life-taking aspects. It is a symbol of the womb within which all life starts, and the tomb where all cycles end.

The Labyrinth in this myth has the fearsome Minotaur at its centre. The original sacred space has been invaded and corrupted by the prevailing culture of King Minos with a fearsome predator placed at the core of what is fundamentally sacred; the life-giving Feminine. Both versions of this labyrinth are in Ariadne's myth and both are present at the same time. Wherever a labyrinth is involved in a story, it is a symbol of an ending, a beginning, or both. Ariadne's life as she has known it, as a girl in her father's kingdom, is over. Layers to this myth through time have created inevitable distortion, so creative licence is required to unpick the layers as best we can.

Relevant here are details and information from another myth. Ariadne's own mother, Pasiphae, gave birth to the Minotaur! The story is that Old King Minos tricked Poseidon, God of the Sea, out of a mighty sacrificial white bull. Poseidon was enraged and took revenge by putting a curse on Old King Minos' wife, Pasiphae. The curse Poseidon put on Pasiphae was to have her fall desperately, passionately and uncontrollably in love with the very same sacred white bull over which he and Minos were at odds. Under Poseidon's curse, Pasiphae burned with sexual desire and lusted for the bull. Overcome, Pasiphae eventually enlisted the help of Daedalus (a skilful craftsman and father of Icarus) to build her a cow within which Pasiphae could disguise herself and so mate with the sacred bull. As luck would have it, she got pregnant.

After the birth of the Minotaur, Old King Minos recruited Daedalus (who had helped Pasiphae) to build the Labyrinth to imprison the Minotaur. Then, in order to bury his own shame and make certain no one would ever know the secret of who the Minotaur was, or how to get out of the Labyrinth (Daedalus knew both of these things), Old King Minos threw Daedalus and his son Icarus into the Labyrinth along with the monster his wife had given birth to. You will remember perhaps that Daedalus and Icarus eventually built wings Daedalus invented, but that too is another story!

Shame partly explains why Ariadne's mother, Pasiphae, is absent in this story. That's what shame does, it "absents" us. The Greek interpretation of the story of Pasiphae and the sacred white bull reduces Pasiphae (who was a more-than-human woman and daughter of the Sun himself) to a stereotyped, vilified emblem of grotesque bestiality who embodied shocking excesses and out of control feminine sensuality. The prevailing culture shamed Ariadne's mother because they feared the results of passions they reviled. It is also of interest that Pasiphae was said to be highly skilled in the arts and ways of herbs. She was a very powerful woman indeed.

Shame has long been a tool of collective patriarchal repression and is present in Western Judeo-Christian cultures. Woman was blamed for loss of the Garden of Eden, and since then women have been made to feel ashamed of their curiosity, their instinctual selves, of their bodies, of their femininity, and also of their spiritual nature. Feminine spirituality is at the core of the sacred wholeness of life, and as a result of having been despised and rejected, most women experience a deep, imposed shame that when it comes to the surface has to be faced.

Is it any wonder Ariadne, sensing the maturing of her own Feminine power, instinctually knows that to survive she must defy her father, Old King Minos, and take her chances running away from home with the help of Theseus? And so in this way, Ariadne leaves her father's house. Ariadne and Theseus, the immature Masculine and Feminine, sail off and away to the island Naxos where their ship stops for the night.

Two great gifts a young woman can have are, firstly, an inner sense of connection to who she is, and secondly a sense of her outer work in the world lying in wait within her. This is included in what Ariadne's Thread symbolises. If a woman isn't connected to her own Thread, she may simply exchange one external identity-defining authority (father) for another (husband, career, children, religion, or nationality). Until such time as a woman develops the courage and capacity to listen for and take action based on the authenticity of her own authority, she will be pulled in directions that don't serve her. Shame and a sense of being fundamentally unworthy disconnect us from the only thing that can save us. Ariadne's Thread.

Facing her fear of the Minotaur and enlisting the help of Theseus, Ariadne stays firmly connected to her Thread. She deals with her fear of what's in the Labyrinth and slays it so that she can leave on her own terms. She has to do this against her father's wishes. This is formative in the development of any young girl who is not to remain a little princess. And **once on Naxos, Ariadne remains faithful to her Thread. She stays on Naxos and does not hook up with Theseus as a replacement for her father.** But we can see why the story gets told that way – culturally it's the prevailing norm. Betrayal is ultimately something we do to ourselves when we're unfaithful to our own intuitive sense of our Thread. In this way, Ariadne is abandoned over and over again in the prevailing narrative of our culture.

Any young woman, who can move through fear and

uncertainty to take steps in the direction of her inner calling, even though it's terrifying, will cross this developmental threshold successfully. Even when things don't turn out the way she hoped (they rarely do), and even if she doesn't get what she thought she wanted, she has been faithful to her Ariadne Thread and it grows stronger and thus easier to keep hold of. Moving out into the world, she's on her own tracks, learning what it means to be central in her own life. She's taken responsibility for her own entelechy, her own unique emergence and begins to build an alternative prevailing context for her own life.

Most of us, at least for a while, lose the thread, the plot in our own lives. The inner Minotaur gets fed with sacrifices of our strength and beauty. Fear can be a relentless driver and "driven doing" is familiar to most Westernised women. Life on a hamster wheel reacting to outer demands and the expectations of the prevailing culture leads to burnout and deep dissatisfaction. It is rampant in our society. It consumes women as surely as the Minotaur did. What's needed is commitment to a different kind of "doing" and "action" that is proactive on behalf of Ariadne rather than reactive to externals. **Action that is always connected, by our Thread, in service of building new ground is the way the Labyrinth is reclaimed.**

The willingness to take action in our own lives and be responsible for the consequences of our actions, without blame and without expecting to be rescued, is Ariadne's journey. And like Ariadne, real life often entangles other people in our Thread and things get messy. But **it's long past time to acknowledge that no one is coming to the rescue.**

Waking up on Naxos – Action, Meaningful Connection and Belonging

The morning after Ariadne leaves home, she wakes up on the island of Naxos and Theseus has left in his ship. Ariadne is alone on new, unfamiliar ground. I doubt there's a woman alive who couldn't tell her own real life "outer" version of this story as a biographical event. But here we're listening for an inner truth. Archetypally, Ariadne is moving from Maiden to Mother and has to access, on her own behalf, what women sometimes access for their children and families. There's a biological shift too that enables her to build a safe place for herself. She has to nourish and keep herself warm. She has to chop wood and haul water on behalf of her own personal development. She has to support herself to stay true to her own unique "Calling" and build a secure and trustworthy inner place for her own Feminine emergence.

If Ariadne knew some version of what had happened to her Mother, consider the impact. Imagine knowing that her Mother's behaviour had resulted in being totally stripped and downgraded to a stereotype of bestiality and deceitfulness. Even with lies and myth entangled here, it isn't hard to see how easily Pasiphae came to represent a cultural warning of what happens when sensuality, sexuality and passion stir a woman. Ariadne's Mother became known throughout the kingdom as "Pasiphae who took pleasure as an adulteress with a bull". Fear and shame have ever been the way to control and dominate the life-giving power of The Feminine. Ariadne is on that same threshold now, stripped of her former place as princess royal in her father's kingdom.

The lie Ariadne was up against is woven through the fabric of life today. Like a double-edged sword, shame and fear can suppress the very instinctive nature and passion that got Ariadne to take creative action and get herself out of the "old" paradigm. If a young woman arriving on Naxos, stripped of her former identity as princess, can't connect to a deeper place in herself to settle in on the beach, she is in danger of betraying herself all over again. It happens time and again if we make choices that abandon Ariadne on the beach. This happens when strong capable women identify exclusively with their inner Theseus, build a ship of their own and sail off on the Hero's Journey stereotyping their inner Ariadne as a victim.

If a woman uses her time of conscious awakening on Naxos simply to build her own ship and teach herself to sail, she abandons her own emerging navigation system, the true north of Ariadne's guiding Thread. In this scenario she ends up serving and being steered by the system she fled. Abandoning her Heroine's Journey on the beach in this way, while a woman may have left the kingdom of Old King Minos physically behind, she has internalised the consciousness and her own awakening is interrupted. When she takes action from that old place, she builds her new life on foundations identical to the world she left. The time on the beach, if she will stay there, is an opportunity at this juncture in the story to build self-worth and a new inner foundation. When Ariadne and Theseus, the Feminine and the Masculine, are equally valued in ourselves we're supported to stay true to the Heroine's Journey.

If as women we value and invest only in our Masculine capacities, and like Theseus, metaphorically study the sea, swordsmanship, ships and as quickly as possible leave the shores of Naxos, The Feminine is sacrificed again and again, in order to protect against a repeat of the devastating emotional experience of betrayal and abandonment. Young women regularly abandon their inner Ariadne and identify with Theseus. It seems there is an inner Minotaur and an inner mess that has to be acknowledged in daily life on new ground.

An alternative narrative is to be found by staying put on the beach. Ariadne's new environment is tidal rhythms, lunar influences on a narrow strip of sand between deep sea and dry land, an intertidal zone where life forms must adapt and evolve to withstand high and low tides. Ariadne is perfectly positioned on the beach to sink deeply into the cyclical and elemental nature of the Mother archetype. She has everything she needs to learn about Feminine creative action and evolve.

The Feminine is a ferocious protectress of cycles of darkness. In the dark, the stark reality of endings and what must be left behind often involves heartbreak and grief. The Feminine acts as a washer away of old ground. The cadence of life on the shore has Ariadne up with first light as dawn breaks and awake to the natural pulse of dying at the end of day. The Labyrinth is slowly cleared and reclaimed as Ariadne reconnects to cycles of birth, death and rebirth as an embodied experience in her daily life.

Absorbed in her new life on Naxos, Ariadne is focused and attentive to rhythms of the Mother archetype, and she roots securely in her new ground. From this rooted place she will in time turn her head and look inland. Her future will emerge from a direction she hadn't previously been aware of or had access to.

Learning to take Feminine action

At least three different kinds of action have been taken so far in this myth. Firstly, there's the intuitive action Ariadne takes from the place of connection to her own Thread to follow her instincts and get away from the Kingdom of Minos.

Secondly, there's the strategic action Ariadne takes when she makes a plan in response to patterns she clearly perceives in her environment. She holds steady with it as she connects with Theseus, communicates it to him and asks him to play his part. Thirdly, there is the warrior-like action Theseus takes and which we're so familiar with in our culture. Theseus executes the plan and performs the dangerous task of taking out and destroying the source of the danger. Warrior-like, he deals with the problem by slaying the Minotaur, and then by using his highly employable skills and tools, he gets them both away from the kingdom of Old King Minos.

The second and third kinds of action are recognised, valued and validated capacities in our culture: the strategic action planning and the warrior action destroying the danger and moving forward. Worth noticing is how rarely these two kinds of action are employed on behalf of Feminine deep listening and the intuitive inner active listening capacity of Ariadne.

There is also a fourth kind of action. Barely understood, other than to conceive, gestate and birth life, this is creative action beyond the biological capacity to physically give birth. The Feminine principle is present in both men and women, but it is in women I believe the ability to reclaim the power of creative action is rooted most securely. It rests in, but is not, the ability to physically give birth.

Creative action supports our own full emergence and that of our vision, projects, talents and power. It supports our sense of new energy, forms and structures that need to be birthed in the world if we are to have a future that is healthy, inclusive and sustainable. However, creative action has, for the most part, been usurped in our culture and put to work by Minos for his own purposes. The power of creative action has all too often been diverted into sustaining the current status quo. This can leave women who have a deep capacity for it, passive rather than active, with respect to taking creative action, in service of what really matters to them.

To take creative action is to act for something, on behalf of something and with something that is emerging, rather than to get something, or remove something that already exists. Creative action works with what isn't yet visible and lets energy, ideas and projects take on a life of their own. **Creative action is committed to the experience of fulfilment rather than the getting of predetermined results.**

This is what Ariadne does on the beach at Naxos, she learns to take creative action on her own behalf. She builds an alternative shelter for her emerging counter narrative and stays there getting strong. She sets up camp on sand that is regularly swept out to sea by tidal forces she has no control over. She learns to work with the tides and natural elements in and around her. It is during this time in a woman's life that she reclaims the sacred nature of the Labyrinth. **If outer action by Theseus was needed to take out the Minotaur, it is inner action by Ariadne that reclaims the Labyrinth.**

If the future is to be different than the past, Ariadne has to be given a permit and authority to set up her beach camp in daily consciousness. She has to be allowed to have a fire on the shore and her primary task is to tend that fire, keep it burning in our awareness. If Ariadne can establish her campsite in our everyday awareness, the next stage of life for a woman unfolds secured, anchored by Ariadne's Thread. Theseus and Ariadne are given time and the conditions in which to mature. Theseus learns to serve a new purpose and work with the subconscious patterns of the sea he sails. Ariadne learns to stay put in her own authority on increasingly solid Feminine ground. She learns about the tides of coming and going that bring cycles of connection with Theseus and his ship in the outer world.

The capacity for Feminine creative action can't be accessed unless we are willing to learn about the power of sitting with our grief for what the tide takes out while we are on the beach. Grieving is an emptying, and on the shore, connected to the tides, Ariadne grieves and is emptied. She grieves the loss of her former life, sense of self, and the previous ordering forces of her perspective. As she does this, she clears and reclaims the power of the labyrinth. Our culture is addicted to numbing the pain of what has been lost. But without reconnection to natural cycles of letting go and grief, there is no healthy womb for new life. The Minotaur causes only more pain, abuse and misuse of resources. The sacred Labyrinth remains a place where waste reigns without Ariadne's cycle of loss and emptying on the beach at Naxos.

During Ariadne's time on the beach she doesn't flee the pain and dark nights. She stays connected to her Thread and learns the lessons that sitting with the unknown has to teach her. She learns that she holds both endings and beginnings in her Thread, and the power of transformation lies in letting go of what doesn't serve her from her past. She moves through her grief, her fear and her anger and, keeping the fire burning for herself, in time, finds joy.

During her beach time on Naxos, whether a woman has had a family, a career, both or something else entirely, in transition, like Ariadne on the shores of Naxos, there is a heightened sense of opportunity to turn inland, away from the known and towards a future that has yet to show itself but is nevertheless emerging. Inland is always there and is where we must go if we are to effectively address the dynamics of our inner family systems or professional networks that need to be raised and brought to maturity. Our inner worlds, just like children, mature over time and are peopled with characters that must learn to work together without domination or abdication. In the work of building this functional inner collaboration and community of characters lies the potential of the true meaning of the gift of Naxos and the shattering of the lie of happily ever after.

Questions to help you reflect on your own experience:

1. Are there any hard truths in your own current life circumstances that need to be spoken?
2. Can you name any contracts that might be structuring your life (a promise you made to yourself, or someone else along the way)?
3. What might you have to let go of if change is to come?
4. What might you have abandoned or betrayed along the way?
5. What do you want to be faithful to at this stage in your life?
6. What's at risk if you let go?
7. What's at risk if you don't let go and the picture stays the same?

Phase Four

Fulfilment, Joy, Blessing and Purpose

The Labyrinth, safe containers and letting go of the way things have been

Dionysus symbol of the mature Masculine principle arrives, in a chariot, which is a symbol of change. In the myth, all this happens in the turn of Ariadne's head. Ariadne's past vanishes over the horizon, and from inland, the opposite direction from which she has come, she sees the chariot arrive out of which leaps the Greek god, Dionysus. Ariadne and Dionysus fall in love, marry and, mutually devoted, they live happily ever after. Dionysus gives Ariadne a crown of stars and Ariadne reclaims her Mother's archetypal place alongside the Gods. Immature Feminine and Masculine have matured and transcend the origins they now leave behind.

Dionysus' origins are blurry. What most agree on is that he is the only god born of a mortal mother. But even that isn't straightforward. Zeus had an affair with a mortal woman called Semele. She died before Dionysus was born and Zeus took the unborn Dionysus and sewed him into his thigh until Dionysus could be released as a fully-grown baby. Another version of his origins has his mother as Persephone and he is killed as a baby by Titans. His heart is saved and is planted in various ways (including Zeus' thigh) from which grows and is born again Dionysus. As a result he is known as the "twice born" and categorised as a dying and rising god. How fitting for a princess restoring Labyrinth Consciousness.

There is a painting by Titian in the National Gallery called *Bacchus and Ariadne* which depicts the moment Dionysus arrives to unite with Ariadne. Greek and Roman mythology regularly get entangled and this is true in Titian's painting. Wild and debauched representations emerge from the woods. Are they a warning or a reward? This is a Roman version all mixed up with the Greek, and Dionysus has become Bacchus. **I can't help wondering if it doesn't reflect and reinforce suspicions that if a woman was to follow her instincts, her bliss, her Ariadne Thread, her life would be dangerously debauched.** It's another example of the ways our Thread of connection has become so profoundly entangled in the outer cultures it has unravelled through over the ages. It's no wonder it's the work of a lifetime to reel in, untangle and do the knotty work of reclaiming our Thread and the fullness of where it takes us if we are willing to follow it.

The integrity of a woman following her "bliss", or Ariadne Thread, has been polluted and is now very far from the original and intended meaning. This is tied up with and reflects our own **present day anxieties and cultural fears of what happens if women step fully into their sense of who they are,** just like Ariadne's mother, Pasiphae. Outer entertainment (the Roman's Bacchus) has replaced the deep pleasure and joy of being fully present to ourselves represented by the union of Ariadne with Dionysus.

Turning inward, inland on the island of Naxos, following Ariadne's Thread and the sound of the genuine, following our "bliss" has once again in Titian's painting been confused with Bacchanalian antics and drunken debauchery. There are so many cultural layers to the myth of Ariadne and Dionysus. Bacchus is a more recent layer supporting the idea of Pasiphae's supposed sexual depravity.

Following Ariadne's Thread and the sound of the genuine in ourselves has everything to do with a deeper experience of creativity, joy and fulfilment. For most women the self-awareness required to reconnect with this is extremely hard won. Women (and men) learn a values system that has nothing to do with valuing The Feminine. Like Ariadne, we grow up in a kingdom with The Feminine supressed and where Pasiphae, the daughter of the Sun himself, is still shamed and reduced to a stereotyped emblem of wanton depravity typifying societal fears and belief about the shocking excesses of female sensuality and sexuality.

Once we connect to what makes us well and whole, we have to hold on. We have to build on that inner foundation and lead from it out into the world the deep truth we find there. This is also what we find at the centre of the true meaning of the Labyrinth: The Holy One, the giver of life; The Feminine. And this is where our story will, finally, intersect with older myths and legends.

Creative action and giving life involve much more than having children and agricultural harvests. The Feminine is the life-giving force, and creativity is fundamentally connected to our ability to walk the Labyrinth through cycles of life, death and rebirth many times in our lives. This is how we exercise our rights to creative renewal.

The arrival of Dionysus brings the supportive inner mature Masculine that enables Ariadne to act in the outer world on her own life-giving and creative behalf. Theseus helped Ariadne to slay the inner Minotaur that would have devoured her creative, life-giving force with familiar devouring voices most of us know only too well: "There's nothing new about your work. Everything you're doing has all been done before and better than you can, so give up. Don't try." Theseus puts a stop to that.

On the beach Ariadne gestates and tends her own inner sense of what her work is in the world. Dionysus arrives to help her manifest her creative instincts in the outer world. Without Dionysus, Ariadne's ideas and projects fall back into becoming Minotaur fodder. Dionysus helps Ariadne feed, raise and nourish her creativity. He takes specific action on her behalf to co-parent her creative offspring and take them out into the world. Once Theseus and Ariadne reclaim the Labyrinth, the dark place becomes once again a place of renewal where the cycles of the creative process unfold and we learn to stay close to its emptiness. In the dark we listen to the sound of the genuine in ourselves, we hear and stay true to our own original voice. **Gestation in the dark** demands we let go of ambition and fixed ideas of results. This is a different terror as we learn to make friends with the true vast emptiness of the Labyrinth and understand the cycles of letting go (not sacrifice), death and renewal.

Ariadne shows the way. She keeps us safe, she keeps us connected. During her time on the beach, she relights a fire she tends faithfully. She nurtures what has been abandoned. She reclaims and rebuilds the archetypal heart(h) fire and protects it from the harsh winds of cultural dismissal. Ariadne's camp on the beach becomes a beacon for others to sail towards. It is an **"Everyday Temple"** and our Heroine's Journey has been more daily pilgrimage than adventure.

At the intersection of inner creative renewal and what the external world around us needs, there is a sweet spot, the birthplace of joy. When we hear our own calling and follow the Thread of it inland, Dionysus shows up and there is much to do of a purposeful, fulfilling and creative nature. We become midwives and mothers for the birth of an emergent future and new dimensions in ourselves and others in what is proving to be a long and difficult birth.

This inner landscape can seem a wild, tangled jungle when we first encounter the edges of it. But as she is drawn inland towards the darker lush vegetation, Ariadne overcomes her fear of loss of her former sense of identity. She transforms the Labyrinth within her. She realises that there is nourishment, comfort and shade in the dark. For Ariadne and for each of us who follow her Thread, our own personal experience of the life, death, rebirth "truth" in daily life is evidence of Labyrinth consciousness at work where the "lie" of the Minotaur once dominated.

Dionysus only shows up once Ariadne has matured and can keep the fire going for herself in her beach camp. This union of mature Masculine and Feminine in us as women gives birth to new ways of being, thinking, and acting so needed in the world today. From this comes blessing and joy in daily life and fulfilment based on values that Ariadne has uncovered for herself. She no longer defines her sense of self or her success in the ways of her father's house, the old patriarchal order. She now stands on her own ground, sovereign in her own realm.

Here and now, we live in a patriarchal context and it is the air we breathe. There are many things we can choose not to do, but we have no choice about breathing. And as we breathe our common air it is an ongoing challenge not to accept elements in our shared air as normal. Because we have no choice about breathing, we inhale toxicity that, as a result, becomes part of us. In the air we breathe, The Feminine is not valued equally. We live and breathe in a patriarchal context and there can be unintended consequences for well-meaning women who want to inspire and guide younger women.

Women who have a good grasp of their own internal Theseus can unintentionally do young women a grave disservice. We risk unconsciously suggesting that helping young Ariadne get away from her father and go off on adventures is the goal in itself. But that is the Hero's Journey, and while Theseus has a crucial role to play, he isn't the point of the story. The point of the story is for Ariadne to reclaim her place alongside Dionysus in a new kingdom.

Adventuring, swashbuckling, outspoken, clever women shine like stars in a very dark sky for young women who are "waiting" on the shores of Naxos. But if we bedazzle them and they are drawn to follow that starlight, they risk losing the true north of Ariadne's Thread because it is firmly laid on the earth. It is an earth-centred, body wisdom thread. If we hold on to our own earthy thread, The Feminine shines with the warmth of spring sunlight bathing a ripening field. Yes, The Feminine is crowned Queen of Heaven, with a circlet of her own stars, but she's very much here on earth with her helpmeet, Greek God Dionysus who was born of a mortal woman.

As the central figure in her own domain, built on an entirely different foundation with a sustainable internal economy of her own, a woman need no longer make deals or trade with the economy of Old King Minos. Ariadne has work to do in our shared outer world to redefine the meaning of work, and success, power and leadership. Once a woman has integrated Dionysus on Naxos she leads the way into an, as yet, unwritten whole new story.

The Labyrinth, creating safe space on the beach, and letting go of the way things have been. Death, birth and renewal

References to labyrinths are universal from prehistory to modern day fascination with them by authors such as Umberto Eco in *The Name of The Rose*. There are labyrinths in cathedrals, Native American designs, Indian designs and Tantric scripts. From places to trap malevolent spirits to symbols of sacred pilgrimage there's a tangled thread of cultural reference.

The Labyrinth as a symbol of the womb we come from and the tomb we go to is a metaphor for the stages of human life and the path we walk on many levels. Each turn the path reveals new directions and during any lifetime there are cycles of birth, death and renewal. This Feminine symbol of "The Mother" also strongly carries the form of placental mass that nourishes unborn life and the tomb of the earth we all return to.

It is understandable how this symbol was corrupted by a dominating patriarchal overlay afraid and threatened by the power represented in this symbol. These days, in our present reality, the symbol of the Labyrinth is being reclaimed in daily life in simple but profound ways. Circles of women come together to provide safe places to stay true to and follow their Ariadne Threads and to learn to let go of what no longer serves them. Women are using these safe places to build resiliency, hold inner ground and stand on it. Supportive contexts are a mighty counterweight to the current patriarchal paradigm. The restored Labyrinth is present in the communication and connection between people when there is safety.

What becomes of broken hearts, I have discovered, depends in part on the calibre of female friendship. When hearts break and shatter, when endings engulf, we have opportunity to hold broken pieces in safety. Sometimes what we cannot find within us we can find between us. And as we tell stories of heartbreak, we can listen for the pieces to take back and reclaim what we may have given away. And we can listen for old versions of our stories we can let go of in the Labyrinth because they don't serve us any longer.

An example of a safe space to journey through heartbreak opened for me when my daughter left home. I was swept up in the annual wave of grief that moves across the country each year in September as young adults take their leave and move out on their own tracks. In spite of the fact that it was everything my daughter and I both wanted, it was also an ending. I was going to miss my daughter. I paid attention, drew wisdom from my inner experience and from outer advice. I wasn't caught off guard. I prepared for when the grief hit as I knew it would. And it did.

In anticipation, I created a safe environment for myself, a Labyrinth, by telling a few people I love and trust that I was going to need them. I told them what time I would be leaving my daughter and that I wanted them to think of us, each starting on her own new path. Driving home alone after leaving my daughter in her new room, I felt connected and supported in ways that mattered to me. Opening the front door when I got home, it was safe to feel my grief.

In the past I might have toughed it out, stoically. But supported, I returned to the original symbolism of the Labyrinth. Had I been isolated, the Minotaur might have devoured me. But supported and connected to threads of love on the outside of my experience I was able to soften and move safely through the natural cycle of ending. I walked the Labyrinth of an in-between time supported through the darkness, shedding and letting go. I walked to the core of meaning in myself following my Ariadne Thread. There was no Minotaur, and I returned to the original meaning of the story experiencing, in time, the ritual of my own rebirth. We can do this for each other in simple, practical ways every day. There was a lot to let go of, and a lot to hold on to, as I completed an extraordinary eighteen-year cycle of child-raising.

Taking responsibility, as best we can, for letting go of past patterns, and experiencing healing at thresholds in life, is one way of describing what we're each here to do. Each of us is the only one who can do our own work. I'm the only person who can pick up a piece of my own story and walk with it through the Labyrinth. It is also true that the edge between devastation and the sweetness of healing and renewal is only as safe as my connection is robust to myself and people who have the capacity to hold safe in the dark. This is the difference between being devoured by the Minotaur and emerging safely, reborn, to start a whole new phase of life.

People who fall down the well of grief and loss, disconnected in the Labyrinth, can shatter. Gentle people, at peace with themselves, understand that heartbreak, grief and pain can be doorways to healing when walked like the journey into a Labyrinth, securely connected to Ariadne's Thread. We need allies who have the capacity to stand lovingly but fiercely on guard at the entrance to the Labyrinth. Entry isn't for the drama hungry or the trauma teams. It's a place for the healers and peacemakers. I am so grateful to women who have stood for me at the entrance to my Labyrinth. Power and grace, courage and companions help make the most of opportunities for letting go and renewal at times of loss and grief in our lives.

Archetypes

Cultural norms all over the world and at different times in human history have produced the same archetypes and related myths. They appear dressed in different costumes depending on the culture they surface in. The differences in the costumes and customs come from environmental and historical conditions. The differences are what anthropologists identify, compare and study. Archetypes, however, embody shared biological truths; they are what we can identify with, cross-culturally, no matter how the archetype is dressed. The costumes and customs are the biographical details that can separate us. The archetypes connect us.

Ariadne as an archetypal biological truth embodies transitions we share. There are some predictable thresholds with hormonal drivers in the development of our stories as women the world over no matter our culture, customs, costumes or religion. Ariadne's story took us through her movement through Maiden to Mother archetype, leaving home and making her own way in the world on Naxos. It is these larger (or deeper) truths that myth powerfully conveys. It can link us to women we thought we had nothing in common with because while the clothes we wear and the language we speak are different, the life thresholds and emotional gateways are shared.

Women can damage each other and distance from each other if we get caught in our different biographical experiences and stereotypes (homemaker vs. career woman) rather than focusing on the biological and archetypal which enable us to see the bigger picture of the multiple roles of womankind and the emergence of The Feminine. We need each other and Ariadne's Thread to reclaim the Labyrinth both in our own lives and in our larger culture.

The weight of patriarchy could be reframed as an enormous pressure bearing down on all of us, men and women. As any woman who has ever given birth knows, considerable pressure is exerted in the process. What we do with the pressure is only partly within our control. The best made birth plans have a way of unravelling in the intensity of what the moment actually requires. But we deal with almost unbearable pressure and intensity most creatively when we are within safe environments we trust.

Questions to help you reflect on your own experience:

1. Is there an aspect of your life where a "safe space" and some support would be helpful?
2. If you felt safe within a challenging situation in your current life, what might you be able to see, think, feel or do?
3. Are there specific ways in which you could create a safe and supportive environment for yourself and others?

Chapter 3

The Lady of the Labyrinth

The prehistory version of the Ariadne myth

Researcher and author Charlene Spretnak differentiates between myths created within patriarchy, and those that predate it. Myths that develop in or pass through patriarchy give limited information about women. What they do best is help us understand how women react under patriarchy. The version we have today of the Ariadne myth is a shattered version. It is what has emerged from reconstructed shards of the story. It is true on the inside with respect to the tale of how every woman deals with, responds to and eventually reacts and attempts to escape and revolt against the prevailing patriarchal paradigm. However, it also points to a deeper truth.

In the prehistory bones of the original story, Ariadne was certainly not a princess. She wasn't even mortal. Ariadne was the name of the Divine, the Great Goddess herself. The name Ariadne means "Most Holy" and Ariadne was revered as the ultimate power, the Great Mother. She was also known as "The Lady of the Labyrinth".

When I went to Knossos in May 2008, it was explained to me by a brilliant local guide that Labyrinth means home of the double X. The symbol X is found engraved on stones in the ruins. Another name for Knossos is "The Palace of the Double X". There is ongoing discussion about what that "Double X" was. Whatever the facts, there is no doubt that Labyrinth has its root in an ancient dialect no longer spoken and that at its root, labyrinth means "home of what is sacred."

In the Labyrinth, the home of what was sacred, lived the Great Mother, Ariadne. She was Goddess, Holy One, and Divine Feminine. She was the embodiment of Feminine wholeness in the culture of Minoan Crete. The Labyrinth was certainly a symbol but may also have been a physical place where people of the time envisioned themselves walking on their journeys, threading their ways through cycles of life, death and rebirth. The role of the goddess, Ariadne, was to guide us and help us through the dark, through the frightening and difficult times of birth and death.

In Minoan Crete there was, according to Riane Eisler, the last surviving example of a pre-patriarchal society. Up until around 1450BC which isn't very long ago, there is evidence of an evolved, enlightened culture with a supreme deity that was female, and women and Feminine values were central and equal. The Labyrinth was a dominant symbol and appears in the art, architecture, stories and sacred ceremonies.

The Labyrinth was a sacred and life-giving symbol. It only became the home of the Minotaur after the fall of the civilization that existed at the time of Minoan Crete. With the suppression of The Feminine, the story reappeared totally transformed with a devouring monster in place of a life-giving womb.

Wherever each of us is in the stages of this myth, the archetypes are all within us, balanced differently because of our unique biology and the biography of our diverse cultures. However, for every woman on the planet, the myth points to the same signposts. It is a call to connect to and integrate our freeing energy, connect to Ariadne's Thread, go into the Labyrinth, slay the Minotaur and get out of thinking in culturally programmed unconscious ways – the ways of the Old King Minos, the patriarchal system. Connect to your inner Theseus. Plan with him to get away. Set up camp on Naxos, let the tides wash away your necessary losses and say goodbye to the aspects of your past that don't serve you. Change your perspective by doing your inner work and becoming self-aware; turn inland.

When we do that, Dionysus arrives. Integrate Dionysus, and

that is where the truth of happily ever after lies and where the new story begins. Once a woman has turned inland and tied the knot of her thread with Dionysus, she begins to establish a whole new sustainable ecology and economy in her daily life. It's a life built on her own balanced values. From this new inner foundation effective leadership by women emerges. It is a leadership of connection and emergence.

And this is where we're at in our collective story. For all the talk of shattering the glass ceiling, all that gives us is equal access to the old patriarchal ways. Our real work is to intuit and invest in life-affirming conditions which redefine the meaning of success and close the chasm between where we are and where we instinctively know we could be. Follow your Thread. The Feminine leadership work of today involves following Ariadne's Thread to the interior of Naxos: sustainable generation and a new economy built on values and worth.

Evidence of the Cretan culture and its ideology reflects a people for whom power had nothing to do with dominance and it's notable that their artwork had no depictions of war or triumph or killing of an enemy. Nor are there any grandiose royals sitting on thrones. It appears there was peace and balance for a very long time.

This story is not intended to be a case to prove anything. Rather, an imaginative call to women to support and trust our instincts. There is an-'other' way and there is companionship on the journey.

Scholarly cases have been written. Books such as Riane Eisler's *The Chalice and the Blade* reconstruct prehistory and offer evidence with respect to how our culture lost its Feminine values. Riane Eisler builds a clear picture in her book of human culture with two models: the dominator model, symbolised by the blade, and the partnership model, symbolised by the life-giving chalice.

So many problems arise with the use of loaded words like

patriarchy and matriarchy. Because we currently live in a world paradigm where parts of society have power "over" others (dominate), we can't easily envision a shift in the balance of power where women won't "dominate" and have power "over" men. What appears to have existed on Minoan Crete was an enlightened equality where men and women worked and lived in partnership with each other and the Earth in a cooperative, collaborative paradigm in which everything was experienced as interconnected.

There is constantly new research in the fields of neuroscience and neurocardiology that supports the possibility of an evolutionary threshold. It seems we may be participating in something that hasn't happened before and perhaps we would do well to remember that extraordinary and earth-shattering things have happened in the history of our planet many times before. For many people, many times, life as they have known it on this planet has come to an end. This isn't the same as life coming to an end.

Chapter 4

Upheaval, sustainability and values

The earthquake and tsunami in Japan on Friday 11th March 2011, and the power of what took place, brought to my mind the stories of Minoan Crete destroyed by a tsunami apparently many times more powerful than the one that wiped out Sendai in Japan. There is growing evidence that Minoan Crete was hit by a tsunami triggered by massive earthquakes and volcanic eruptions to the north of the island on what was then Thera. It is now known as Santorini and you can visit the volcano. The contents of the volcano were dumped into the sea and this triggered the unimaginable tsunami that destroyed life as it had been. That it wiped out a civilization isn't disputed. What is disputed is what Minoan Crete was. Was it a global economy built on Feminine values of partnership that were woven through with reverence for the earth? Was the earth revered as the body of the great Mother giving birth to bounty and abundance that sustained the people? Whatever was present, its destruction was part of the resulting collapse of the prevailing cultural paradigm on the planet at that time.

The collapse of the financial and banking system in 2008 and the economic recession in much of the Western world is ongoing. In India and China there has been a demand to be allowed to "catch up" with all the "taking" the economies of the West have already done, polluting and destroying our environment in the process. This is the truly entrenched Minos "dominator" patriarchal paradigm. It is not sustainable, and as arguments rage about if global warming is man-made or a naturally occurring part of the cycles of the earth, there is still an assumption that Western economies will recover and boom again. But what if they don't?

Other changes taking place make it possible to begin to articulate another way. Women who reach midlife and stop to look at their lives and what they value are adding impetus to a swelling tsunami of a different kind, in part, a hormonal tide. I hear it every day, "There must be another way, surely there is more."

There are enormous challenges when everyday women like me pick up Ariadne's Thread and follow it. The main challenge I personally have to face is the gap between what I sense could be done, and the here and now reality of what I can actually accomplish.

A bumper sticker from years ago read "I wanted to change the world but I couldn't find a babysitter." Even if we do find a great babysitter (or even if we have no children), the chasm between the roles we sense we want to play and the reality of daily life can defeat us before we even get started. This is why it is, from my perspective, so important for women to have safe spaces to connect, share, really hear each other and ultimately find the support to take creative action. While each of us can only take hold of Ariadne's Thread for ourselves, we lead the way for more than ourselves and is the only way I'm currently aware of to end up somewhere we might want to be.

Each woman must become self-reliant by turning inland and integrating her own values rather than looking outward for the next passing ship. She must become an exporter of her own sustainable generation and give up, once and for all, any lingering longing for value to be bestowed upon her, imported somehow, from an external economy and values system that is failing and never actually worked in her interests.

Until such a time that guiding Feminine principles are integrated into our global economic policies, we will have to experiment with this ourselves in imaginative and creative ways.

Chapter 5

Redefining success on our own terms

Many women are stepping back and taking time out to deeply consider what success means to them very personally at different ages and stages of their lives. What are the things that really matter? And what combination and balance of those things enable an experience of being a successful woman? **By clearly defining success on personally sustainable terms and being willing to "fail" in the old paradigm, we begin to experience what it means to be true to ourselves.**

Connected to Ariadne's Thread while engaged in our daily lives there's an authentic sense of serving a purpose and doing what is ours to do. While things may not be easy, challenges are experienced as a creative tension rather than as stress. There is a sense of acting in service of what is life-giving and meaningful. Disconnected from Ariadne's Thread, external forces pull and compete for our energy, that's stress. It is debilitating, drags us down and makes us sick.

Young women need the support of wise women to help them untangle their own Thread without being pulled and distracted by the tugging of mainstream values that do not serve them. Once a girl is severed from her own sense of inner guidance and passion (the Minotaur at work), becoming subsumed in the lives of others and putting the needs of others first easily follows. Other people who know what they want seem to have urgent and important needs.

I hear women in their 30s and 40s say in a variety of ways: "I don't know what I need. I'm just tired." They have become what Sue Monk Kidd in her book *The Dance of the Dissident Daughter* calls "revolving women" who have lost their own anchor in themselves. They revolve around other well anchored people serving their needs and helping them achieve their goals. One of the greatest and most challenging things to ask a revolving woman to do is to just stand still.

If a revolving woman can overcome her own fear of standing still (because she feels she might just float away without an anchor of her own) very often there is a roar of protest from the people and organisations who count on her to support them. Hormones too play a role in this journey and it is very often when a woman moves into perimenopause that she grows weary enough to realise that something has to change. Yet again, hormones have a role to play at this stage.

For a woman who has put the needs of others in place of her own sense of primacy in her own life and world, menopause can be an alarm(ing) clock. The patriarchal paradigm has little use for an aging woman losing her fertility, her looks and her willingness (supported by her hormones) to support and serve the needs of other people.

Calling and inner enrichment versus an outer job and money

Without forgetting that Theseus and Ariadne are the maturing Feminine and maturing Masculine at work in all women, they are at work together in service of building a new context; Ariadne on the beach and Theseus at sea in his ship. Women are currently playing a leading role in the evolving dynamics of work and reward, achievement and success (for both men and women) in our culture. Many women are finding that in the process of leading "successful" lives professionally using Theseus skills, vital aspects of their creativity and intelligence (Ariadne) remain at best underemployed, at worst abandoned on the beach.

Despite significant external recognition and achievement for many women, hunger for alternative, sustainable ways to build meaningful lives is on the rise. Not so long ago, there was something noble about the desire to "better ourselves", but that desire has become corrupted in our culture, separated from its original meaning in much the same way as money has become separated from worth. In the dominant culture of Old King Minos, "bettering ourselves" has come to mean extracting as much as we can for ourselves.

The original meaning included enrichment, inwardly. Enrichment also includes valuing a sense of personal Calling and a wish to lead an outer life from an inner sense of connection to what we have to give. This is rooted in a sense of abundance, not scarcity. This is a profoundly Feminine approach to taking creative action. It comes from a sense of having something to offer rather than something to get rid of, or something to get.

The meaning of "bettering ourselves" has come away from its true meaning of finding support to move through a creative process that nurtures an inner seed, gestates it and births it. This original idea of "bettering ourselves" has been replaced by a sense that something is missing, and earning or owning more will "fix" it. But nothing "out there" will "fix" this. Needing a "fix" just feeds an addiction, like painkillers to avoid feeling the terror of the appetite of an insatiable inner Minotaur.

Evidence is all around us of an unconnected Theseus being put to work on his own, disconnected from Ariadne and her Thread. Those who are paid the most are rarely people we would point to and agree contribute the most value and worth in society. And those we can point to and agree are contributing huge value and worth are most often paid very little, if at all. Money has become divorced from worth and value.

If "bettering" our lives as women is driven by "doing" and if we take action disconnected from Ariadne's Thread, Theseus is out there on his own again and Ariadne is stranded on the beach. We perpetuate the "disconnect" in this way and money does not guarantee feeling rich or safe. Naxos is where we stake out our inner ground and clean up our own inner environment.

We redefine success on our own terms. Theseus learns to do his work in the world, connected to Ariadne, and doing our "work" in the world becomes a transformative part of new ground that is emerging.

Chapter 6

The New Story

New perspective on this ancient myth might help us rewrite our current narratives as women. We're still the same people, it's still the same world, but new insight on our own stories allows us to experience them in new ways. The way we tell our stories matters. Remembering that a myth is true on the inside but not necessarily factual on the outside, we begin to see that inner faithfulness each day to the new life on Naxos has outer world impact. When that faithfulness is in place, Dionysus can show up and begin to play his part and do some of our inner heavy lifting. Our work is the same but we are so much better equipped to do it.

The commitments we make with respect to another person in marriage ceremonies, or any relationship, are proven first with respect to our own personal inner cast of characters. What of a new inner marriage? How about a pronouncement of devotion to honour one's soul, to have and to hold, for better or for worse, in sickness and in health?

The nautical definition of *marry* is "to join two ropes end to end by interweaving their strands". Theseus and Ariadne had to do that to defeat the Minotaur. The interweaving between the life of our spirits, our psychology and our biology is ongoing. Our humanness and our archetypal energy create a marriage, a supportive undergirding capable, like the joined ropes, of bearing us through the hard work of reclaiming the Labyrinth.

There aren't many facts to support the story I am telling. I have to take authority from the truth of my own experience. My invitation is for you to do the same. Follow your thread, tell your story and lead your life with your own experience informing your next steps. And revisit interpretations of the old stories.

Question them. Check on your orientation and ensure you are married to your inner authority, not tangled in outer norms that don't serve you.

There is historical and archaeological evidence available to support a new narrative of the emerging Feminine as a guiding story into our future. Author Charlene Spretnak in her book *Lost Goddesses of Early Greece* suggests taking great care when we read myths. She cautions us to be sure to consider the context within which they evolved. There are myths that were created within patriarchy and there are also myths that predate our records of history and predate patriarchy.

There are cultures and civilizations that existed before our records began. While the evidence of them is very limited, an even bigger problem is that when the scant evidence is examined and searched for meaning, it is done so from the frame of our current world view, or paradigm. This means that the point of what we're looking at is truly at risk of being missed. This is because we tend to project on to others whatever our own views and assumptions are. This has been true for scholars and archaeologists looking to reconstruct our prehistory using the very little surviving data and evidence there is.

It's not hard to imagine how easy a mistake it would be for an ancient depiction of a sheaf of wheat to be seen as arrows if the assumption is that peoples, prehistory, were only ever primitive and warlike. Riane Eisler explains at length in her book *The Chalice and the Blade* that the reconstruction of prehistory is difficult not just because we lack many of the pieces, but mostly because our current and prevailing paradigm makes it all but impossible to see the pieces that have survived for what they actually are and imagine a pattern or system into which they fit. Immense pieces of the past have been thoroughly shattered. The systemic lens through which we might see the deeper truths needs refocusing.

The challenge for women today is exactly this. As both our

biographies and our biology push (supported by our hormones at each stage of our lives) for changes in the way we experience ourselves, there isn't the context to make sense of what's emerging. Our stories may each be different but what serves all of us is having safe spaces to tell them. In a safe space there's increased support to follow the Thread. In a safe space it's easier to see how individual Threads weave new patterns and new systems become visible that can begin to offer solutions to many of the complex challenges we can all identify today.

This story provides one lens through which to identify some of the invisible but powerful archetypal forces that drive behaviour. It is one lens through which to engage the systemic influences of our past and gain access to old stories that might enable personal insight and breakthroughs. When we fully include our own inner cast of characters we disentangle from our own dysfunctional ways of relating to the outer world.

With an inner marriage of Feminine and Masculine, all our outer relationships change. Whatever the truth of happily ever after is, holding on to Ariadne's Thread and following it leads always in surprising and unexpected directions. The truth on the inside of myths from the past helps to reimagine a future in which the Creative Process is honoured and Labyrinth Consciousness is restored.

Women have learned to struggle and to consider surrender a dirty word; Ariadne's myth is the story of women's struggle within patriarchy. But it is also a new story of surrender to the focused dynamism of the Masculine working in partnership with the engaged creativity of The Feminine. Active surrender to the Thread of our own becoming leads a trustworthy way through the dark. With commitment to an inner marriage in our daily lives, at each threshold we cross we discover a little more about the truth of happily ever after.

For now, my life (and yours) goes on. But one day, my actual life will end. This is not the same as the end of life. Happily, life itself goes on, ever after; but certainly not as we've known it. Nothing and no one lives for ever. But in the Labyrinth restored, we walk reconnected and secure in a creative process. In a sacred cycle of giving and returning we are guided through the dark of beginnings and endings. Happily, there is... life ever after.

THE END

References and Resources

Acknowledgements
Sue Monk Kidd, *The Dance of the Dissident Daughter*
Charlene Spretnak, *Lost Goddesses of Early Greece*
Riane Eisler, *The Chalice and the Blade*
Louann Brizendine MD, *The Female Brain*
Joseph Chilton Pearce, *The Biology of Transcendence*
Angeles Arrien, *The Second Half of Life*
Barbara Cecil, "The Symbols Way", for the inspiration and structure of the questions

Quotes and citations
1. Koffka quote: Heider, F. 1977. Cited in Dewey, RA, 2007. *Psychology: An Introduction*: Chapter Four – "The Whole is Other than the Sum of the Parts". Retrieved 4/12/2014.
   https://academia.stackexchange.com/questions/83407/how-to-cite-this-quote-the-whole-is-other-than-the-sum-of-its-parts-in-an-arti
2. Longitudinal Study of Young People in England:
   https://www.gov.uk/government/uploads/system/uploads/attachment_data/file/599871/LSYPE2_w2-research_report.pdf
3. Jean Shinoda Bolen in the introduction to her book *Goddesses in Older Women* (page xxv)

At the end of this part of our journey
Thank you for reading these words. My wish is that, as she did for me, Ariadne has connected you more robustly to your own Thread. It's always there, and so is She. This slim volume is an expression of trust in the truth of experience. It may well be the only guide we'll have on the uncertain road ahead.

If you would like to know about workshops and programs I run for women, there are several ways to be in touch. I am also working on another myth and will let you know when it's ready if you'd like to sign up to my mailing list which you'll find on my website. My blog is there too.

And finally, if you have a few moments, please consider adding your review of this book at your favourite online site for feedback. With thanks on the journey, Sarah-Jane

Author's Biography

Having lived, worked and raised her daughter in a number of different countries that include America, France, Italy and South Africa, Sarah-Jane Menato now lives in the UK and runs her own Gloucestershire-based coaching, personal and leadership development consultancy. She offers coaching to individuals and groups, specialising in working with women to define success on their own terms and build lives of authenticity and fulfilment.

Sarah-Jane is committed to supporting individuals and groups as they identify and integrate core values and express them in everyday life. She has thirty years of experience inspiring people to take a stand for the quality of their daily lives and their communities.

A graduate of The Coaches Training Institute's Advanced Co-Active Coaching Program in the US, Sarah-Jane is also trained and experienced in Dr M. Scott Peck's Community Building Model and a graduate of The Community Facilitation Program. She has a Counselling Certificate from the University of London's Birkbeck College and is an experienced Open Space Technology facilitator. She is also dual certified by the ICF and Centre for Systemic Constellations as a coach and systemic practitioner.

Sarah-Jane works with individuals and organisations in the process of change. She supports and encourages life sustaining environments within which new options, possibilities and innovations can emerge.

Website: www.sjmcoachingandtraining.co.uk
Twitter: @sarahjanemenato
LinkedIn: Sarah-Jane Menato

O-BOOKS

SPIRITUALITY

O is a symbol of the world, of oneness and unity; this eye
represents knowledge and insight. We publish titles on general
spirituality and living a spiritual life. We aim to inform and
help you on your own journey in this life.
If you have enjoyed this book, why not tell other readers
by posting a review on your preferred book site? Recent
bestsellers from O-Books are:

Heart of Tantric Sex
Diana Richardson
Revealing Eastern secrets of deep love and intimacy to Western
couples.
Paperback: 978-1-90381-637-0 ebook: 978-1-84694-637-0

Crystal Prescriptions
The A-Z guide to over 1,200 symptoms and their healing
crystals
Judy Hall
The first in the popular series of six books, this handy little
guide is packed as tight as a pill-bottle with crystal remedies
for ailments.
Paperback: 978-1-90504-740-6 ebook: 978-1-84694-629-5

Rising in Love
My Wild and Crazy Ride to Here and Now, with Amma, the
Hugging Saint
Ram Das Batchelder
Rising in Love conveys an author's extraordinary journey of
spiritual awakening with the Guru, Amma.
Paperback: 978-1-78279-687-9 ebook: 978-1-78279-686-2

Thinker's Guide to God
Peter Vardy
An introduction to key issues in the philosophy of religion.
Paperback: 978-1-90381-622-6

Your Simple Path
Find happiness in every step
Ian Tucker
A guide to helping us reconnect with what is really important
in our lives.
Paperback: 978-1-78279-349-6 ebook: 978-1-78279-348-9

365 Days of Wisdom
Daily Messages To Inspire You Through The Year
Dadi Janki
Daily messages which cool the mind, warm the heart and guide
you along your journey.
Paperback: 978-1-84694-863-3 ebook: 978-1-84694-864-0

Body of Wisdom
Women's Spiritual Power and How it Serves
Hilary Hart
Bringing together the dreams and experiences of women across
the world with today's most visionary spiritual teachers.
Paperback: 978-1-78099-696-7 ebook: 978-1-78099-695-0

Dying to Be Free
From Enforced Secrecy to Near Death to True Transformation
Hannah Robinson
After an unexpected accident and near-death experience,
Hannah Robinson found herself radically transforming her life,
while a remarkable new insight altered her relationship with
her father, a practising Catholic priest.
Paperback: 978-1-78535-254-6 ebook: 978-1-78535-255-3

The Ecology of the Soul
A Manual of Peace, Power and Personal Growth for Real People
in the Real World
Aidan Walker
Balance your own inner Ecology of the Soul to regain your
natural state of peace, power and wellbeing.
Paperback: 978-1-78279-850-7 ebook: 978-1-78279-849-1

Not I, Not other than I
The Life and Teachings of Russel Williams
Steve Taylor, Russel Williams
The miraculous life and inspiring teachings of one of the
World's greatest living Sages.
Paperback: 978-1-78279-729-6 ebook: 978-1-78279-728-9

On the Other Side of Love
A Woman's Unconventional Journey Towards Wisdom
Muriel Maufroy
When life has lost all meaning, what do you do?
Paperback: 978-1-78535-281-2 ebook: 978-1-78535-282-9

Readers of ebooks can buy or view any of these bestsellers by clicking on the live link in the title. Most titles are published in paperback and as an ebook. Paperbacks are available in traditional bookshops. Both print and ebook formats are available online.

Find more titles and sign up to our readers' newsletter at
http://www.johnhuntpublishing.com/mind-body-spirit

Follow us on Facebook at https://www.facebook.com/OBooks/
and Twitter at https://twitter.com/obooks